MODERN BAND METHOD

Ukulele

Book 1

Kris Gilbert
Scott Burstein
Spencer Hale
Mary Claxton
Dave Wish

Contributors:

Tony Sauza, Clayton McIntyre, Lauren Brown, Joe Panganiban

To access audio and video visit:
www.halleonard.com/mylibrary

Enter Code
6548-0846-4368-5772

ISBN 978-1-7051-6922-3

HAL•LEONARD®

Visit Hal Leonard Online at
www.halleonard.com

Contact us:
Hal Leonard
7777 West Bluemound Road
Milwaukee, WI 53213
Email: info@halleonard.com

In Europe, contact:
Hal Leonard Europe Limited
1 Red Place
London, W1K 6PL
Email: info@halleonardeurope.com

In Australia, contact:
Hal Leonard Australia Pty. Ltd.
4 Lentara Court
Cheltenham, Victoria, 3192 Australia
Email: info@halleonard.com.au

Introduction

Welcome!

If you are reading this, you have already made the decision to learn to play the ukulele so that you can play some of your favorite songs. One of the best things about playing in a Modern Band is that you don't need much time to start jammin', but there are plenty of skills to learn and master over time too. Most popular musicians are able to perform in a wide variety of musical styles by playing chords with different rhythms to accompany a vocalist. They often add memorable **riffs**, or short melodic phrases, that stay in your head all day. This method book is designed to teach you skills to play the ukulele and create music in a variety of popular music styles—pop, rock, R&B, funk, hip-hop, and more. Let's get started!

Jam Tracks 🔊 and Video Lessons ▶

Use the audio Jam Tracks throughout this book to practice the songs and exercises. Also be sure to watch the included video lessons that demonstrate many of the techniques and concepts. To access all of the audio and video files for download or streaming, just visit *www.halleonard.com/mylibrary* and enter the code found on page 1 of this book.

Parts of the Ukulele

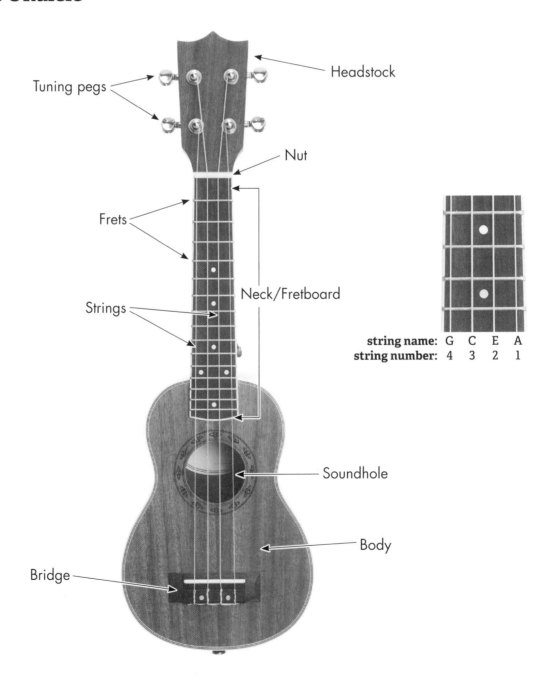

string name: G C E A
string number: 4 3 2 1

Tuning ▶

Even if you're using perfect technique, your ukulele won't sound right if it's not in tune. Be sure to watch the video and tune your ukulele before you start playing.

Basic Technique ▶

Hold the neck of the ukulele in your left hand and use the inside of your right forearm to hold the body of the ukulele against your body. If you're standing, hold it the same way. You can also use a strap for standing (or sitting), which makes it easier to hold the instrument. If your ukulele has been restrung to use it left-handed, use the opposite hands.

You can play notes by strumming with your thumb or pointer (index) finger over the bottom of the fretboard, or by plucking the strings with your fingers. Do what is comfortable for you.

If you are choosing to strum with your pointer finger, position your fingers as if counting the number 1, turn your hand with your palm facing you, and position your hand and arm in front of the ukulele. Curl your pointer finger slightly and use the nail to gently brush across the strings in a downward motion. If you are using your thumb, gently strum with the side of your thumb by your thumbnail. Whichever finger you use, keep it relaxed.

Notation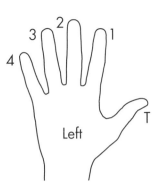

The fingers of the left hand (the fretting hand for a right-handed ukulele player) are numbered 1–4, starting with the pointer finger:

Here are a few graphics that will show up throughout each section. The first is the **chord diagram**. The numbers in the circles refer to the left-hand fingers used to press down the strings. The open circles tell you to play a string **open**, or without holding down any frets. If you see an "X" over a string, it means to not play that string.

Emi

Strumming

Next, let's look at how we notate rhythms. Count these numbers steadily, "1, 2, 3, 4, 1, 2, 3, 4...," and strum down on the black numbers. Strumming on the numbers is called playing the "on-beats."

1	2	3	4

1	2	3	4

The "+" signs (spoken as "and") between numbers are called "off-beats." When playing these, strum up toward your face rather than down toward the ground.

1	2	3 + 4

1 + 2 + 3	4

Learning rhythms and chords will improve your ability to "comp." **Comping** means using your musical knowledge to make up rhythms over a chord progression that fit a song's style.

This book is designed for you to learn alongside other Modern Band musicians so you can jam with your friends and classmates, but it can also be used as a stand-alone book to learn to play the ukulele. Though some of the skills that you will be working on during each section will be different from those of the other instruments, all of the Full Band Songs are designed to be played by a whole band together. Now, let's start playing some music!

In the Modern Band Method series, this section is unique to the ukulele, designed to give some basic chords and initial practice Jam Tracks. If you are using this book in a class with other Modern Band instruments, the exercises will begin to line up with the other books in Section 1. The following songs are transposed to keys that work well for beginning ukulele chords.

Beginning Chords: C, Ami, F

To play the C major chord, place the third finger of your left hand on the 3rd fret of the 1st string and strum all the strings. (Note: Chord symbols for major chords use only the letter; for instance, C major is just "C." Chord symbols for minor chords use the letter and "mi"; so, A minor is "Ami.")

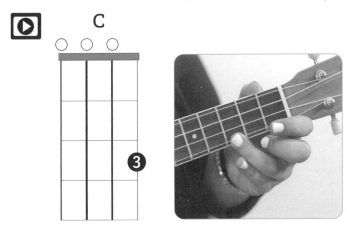

To play the A minor chord (Ami), place your left-hand middle finger on the 2nd fret of the 4th string and strum all the strings.

To play the F major chord (F), start by fretting the Ami chord; then, add the first finger of your left hand to the 1st fret of the 2nd string without touching the other strings. Use your fingertips—not the pads of your fingers—to fret the strings.

For now, use the following patterns to practice strumming these chords. Count to four and strum down (indicated by the symbol ⊓) on every black beat. Don't play the grey beats. Repeat these patterns over and over without pausing.

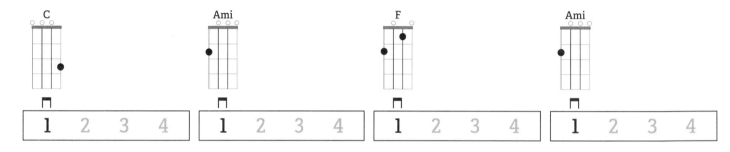

Now, let's play some songs!

CAN'T STOP THE FEELING! 🔊
Justin Timberlake

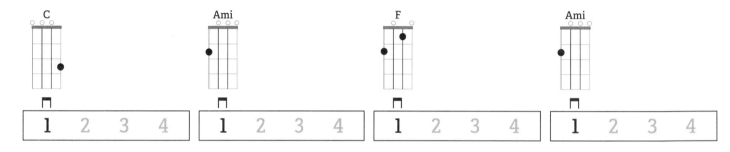

Another way music is written is with the names of the chords above the song lyrics. This type of chart doesn't tell you how many beats to play each chord, but it shows you which lyrics to sing when the chords change. Play C when you sing "feeling" and switch to Ami on the word "bones."

          C   Ami
I've got this feeling inside my bones.

        F   Ami
It goes electric, wavy when I turn it on.

          C   Ami
All through my city, all through my home,

        F   Ami
We're flying up, no ceiling, when we in our zone.

        C   Ami
I got that sunshine in my pocket, got that good soul in my feet.

        F   Ami
I feel that hot blood in my body when it drops, ooh.

        C   Ami
I can't take my eyes up off it, moving so phenomenally.

        F   Ami
Room on lock the way we rock it, so don't stop.

from TROLLS
Words and Music by Justin Timberlake, Max Martin and Shellback
Copyright © 2016 by Universal Music - Z Tunes LLC, Tennman Tunes, DWA Songs, MXM and KMR Music Royalties II SCSp
All Rights for Tennman Tunes Administered by Universal Music - Z Tunes LLC
All Rights for DWA Songs Administered by Universal Music Corp.
All Rights for MXM and KMR Music Royalties II SCSp Administered Worldwide by Kobalt Songs Music Publishing
International Copyright Secured   All Rights Reserved

Here are some other songs that use the same three chords: Ami, C, and F. In the first two songs, each chord is played for eight beats.

WITHOUT YOU
David Guetta ft. Usher

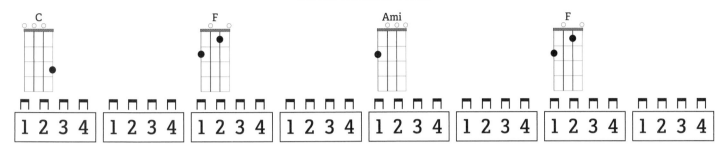

C
I can't win, I can't reign. I will never win this game **F** without you, **Ami** without **F** you.

C
I am lost, I am vain. I will never be the same **F** without you, **Ami** without **F** you.

C
I won't run, I won't fly. I will never make it by **F** without you, **Ami** without **F** you.

C
I can't rest, I can't fight. All I need is you and I, **F** without you, **Ami** without **F** you.

SEND MY LOVE (TO YOUR NEW LOVER) 🔊
Adele

C
This was all you, none of it me. You put your hands on, on my body and told me, **Ami**

you told me you were ready

C
For the big one, for the big jump. I'd be your last love, everlasting, you and me. **Ami**

That was what you told me.

C
I'm giving you up, I've forgiven it all. You set me **Ami** free.

C
Send my love to your new lover, treat her better.

Ami
We've gotta let go of all of our ghosts. We both know we ain't kids no more.

C
Send my love to your new lover, treat her better.

Ami
We've gotta let go of all of our ghosts.
We both know we ain't kids no more.

In this song, the Ami and F chords are played for two beats each, and then C is played for four beats.

WAKE ME UP 🔊
Avicii ft. John Legend

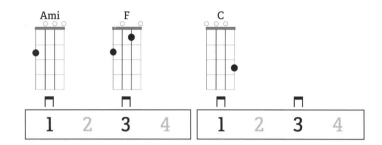

Ami   **F**   **C**
Feeling my way through the darkness,

Ami   **F**   **C**
Guided by a beating heart.

Ami   **F**   **C**
I can't tell where the journey will end,

Ami   **F**   **C**
But I know where to start.

Ami   **F**   **C**
They tell me I'm too young to understand.

Ami   **F**   **C**
They say I'm caught up in a dream.

Ami   **F**   **C**
Well, life will pass me by if I don't open up my eyes.

Ami   **F**   **C**
Well, that's fine by me.

       Ami   **F**   **C**
So wake me up when it's all over,

     Ami   **F**   **C**
When I'm wiser and I'm older.

      Ami   **F**   **C**
All this time I was finding myself

Ami   **F**   **C**
And I didn't know I was lost.

Words and Music by Aloe Blacc, Tim Bergling and Michael Einziger
Copyright © 2011, 2013 Aloe Blacc Publishing, Inc., EMI Music Publishing Scandinavia AB,
Universal Music Corp. and Elementary Particle Music
All Rights for Aloe Blacc Publishing, Inc. Administered Worldwide by Kobalt Songs Music Publishing
All Rights for EMI Music Publishing Scandinavia AB Administered by Sony Music Publishing (US) LLC,
424 Church Street, Suite 1200, Nashville, TN 37219
All Rights for Elementary Particle Music Administered by Universal Music Corp.
All Rights Reserved   Used by Permission

For Ukulele Only

Since this book is designed to be used with the other Modern Band Method books, you will be learning the G and E minor (Emi) chords earlier than usual. These ukulele chords can be more difficult for some beginners, so alternative solutions are provided below. Though the rest of the book includes the full versions of these chords, you can always refer back here for the alternative options, which include fewer fretted notes and adjusted fingerings. It is important to choose what is most comfortable for you.

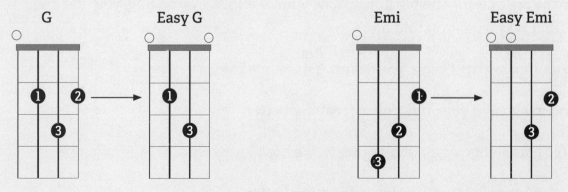

Notice that the 3rd finger can remain anchored when switching from Easy G to Easy Emi and Easy Emi to Easy G!

SECTION 1

Playing Chords: One-Chord Jam 🔊

Play the E minor chord by placing your pointer finger on the 2nd fret of the 1st string, your middle finger on the 3rd fret of the 2nd string, and your ring finger on the 4th fret of the 3rd string. You also have the option of using the Easy Emi chord, as shown in Section A. Do what is most comfortable for you.

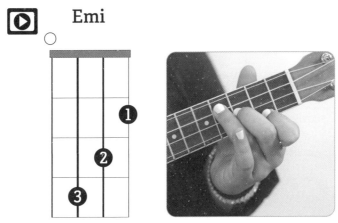

Emi

Try out the new chord with the same strum patterns you played before. Remember to count to four and strum down (⊓) on every black beat. Don't play the grey beats.

⊓					⊓		⊓			⊓	⊓	⊓	⊓
1	2	3	4		**1**	2	**3**	4		**1**	**2**	**3**	**4**

Now, try these strum patterns with another new chord. If you need to use the Easy G chord, refer back to the end of Section A.

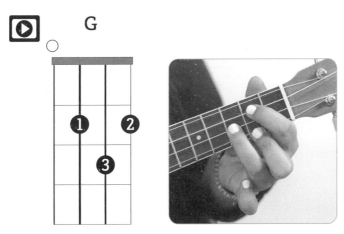

G

Improvisation: Two-Note Solo 🔊 ▶

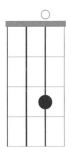

To **improvise** is to spontaneously create music. The two notes shown here can be used to improvise a solo—the open 2nd string, which is the note E, and the 3rd fret on the 2nd string, which is the note G. Unlike the chord diagrams, this image shows two notes that you can play on the ukulele, but not at the same time.

Practice playing these two notes in a variety of ways by mixing up the rhythm and order. Here are some ideas for improvisation:
- Start by playing the open note twice and switching to the G.
- Alternate between the two notes rapidly and then slowly. Then, try changing speeds.
- Focus on rhythm and lock in with the Jam Track.
- Play a rhythm on just the E, and then repeat that rhythm on the G.

Music Theory: The Song Chart

One way music is written is with a **lead sheet**. A lead sheet tells a musician how to play the chords of a song. The lead sheet example below has four **measures** (or **bars**), which are divided by vertical lines (**bar lines**). Each measure is made up of four beats, shown by the diagonal lines, or **slashes** (/). You can play any four-beat strum patterns over those four beats. The measures are repeated over and over again, indicated by the **repeat bar**.

The next part of the lead sheet is the chords. The song below uses a G chord for four beats (one measure), then an Emi chord for four beats, a C chord for four beats, and finally another Emi chord for four beats. The song then repeats that pattern over and over again, indicated by the repeat bars.

CAN'T STOP THE FEELING!
Justin Timberlake

Here is the same song presented in the lyrics and chords format you played earlier, but now with the new chords you've learned.

      G   **Emi**
I've got this feeling inside my bones.

      C   **Emi**
It goes electric, wavy when I turn it on.

      G   **Emi**
All through my city, all through my home,

      C   **Emi**
We're flying up, no ceiling, when we in our zone.

      G   **Emi**
I got that sunshine in my pocket, got that good soul in my feet.

      C   **Emi**
I feel that hot blood in my body when it drops, ooh.

      G   **Emi**
I can't take my eyes up off it, moving so phenomenally.

      C   **Emi**
Room on lock the way we rock it, so don't stop.

Next, try the other songs you already played in Section A with the new chords. In the first two songs, each chord is played for eight beats.

WITHOUT YOU 🔊
David Guetta ft. Usher

G   C   Emi   C

‖: / / / / | / / / / | / / / / | / / / / | / / / / | / / / / | / / / / | / / / / :‖

⊓ ⊓ ⊓ ⊓
1 2 3 4

G   C   Emi   C
I can't win, I can't reign. I will never win this game without you, without you.

G   C   Emi   C
I am lost, I am vain. I will never be the same without you, without you.

G   C   Emi   C
I won't run, I won't fly. I will never make it by without you, without you.

G   C   Emi   C
I can't rest, I can't fight. All I need is you and I, without you, without you.

SEND MY LOVE (TO YOUR NEW LOVER) 🔊
Adele

G   Emi

‖: / / / / | / / / / | / / / / | / / / / | / / / / | / / / / | / / / / | / / / / :‖

⊓ ⊓ ⊓ ⊓
1 2 3 4

G   Emi
This was all you, none of it me. You put your hands on, on my body and told me,
      you told me you were ready

G   Emi
For the big one, for the big jump. I'd be your last love, everlasting, you and me.
      That was what you told me.

G   Emi
I'm giving you up, I've forgiven it all. You set me free.

G
Send my love to your new lover, treat her better.

     Emi
We've gotta let go of all of our ghosts. We both know we ain't kids no more.

G
Send my love to your new lover, treat her better.

     Emi
We've gotta let go of all of our ghosts.
     We both know we ain't kids no more.

In this song, the Emi and C chords are played for two beats each, and then G is played for four beats.

WAKE ME UP

Avicii ft. John Legend

Emi | C | G

‖: / / / / | / / / / :‖

☐ ☐
1 2 **3** 4

Emi   **C**   **G**
Feeling my way through the darkness,

Emi   **C**   **G**
Guided by a beating heart.

Emi   **C**   **G**
I can't tell where the journey will end,

Emi **C**   **G**
But I know where to start.

Emi   **C**   **G**
They tell me I'm too young to understand.

Emi   **C**   **G**
They say I'm caught up in a dream.

Emi   **C**   **G**
Well, life will pass me by if I don't open up my eyes.

Emi   **C**   **G**
Well, that's fine by me.

                 Emi   **C**   **G**
So wake me up when it's all over,

             Emi **C**   **G**
When I'm wiser and I'm older.

           Emi   **C**   **G**
All this time I was finding myself

Emi   **C**   **G**
And I didn't know I was lost.

Words and Music by Aloe Blacc, Tim Bergling and Michael Einziger
Copyright © 2011, 2013 Aloe Blacc Publishing, Inc., EMI Music Publishing Scandinavia AB,
Universal Music Corp. and Elementary Particle Music
All Rights for Aloe Blacc Publishing, Inc. Administered Worldwide by Kobalt Songs Music Publishing
All Rights for EMI Music Publishing Scandinavia AB Administered by Sony Music Publishing (US) LLC,
424 Church Street, Suite 1200, Nashville, TN 37219
All Rights for Elementary Particle Music Administered by Universal Music Corp.
All Rights Reserved Used by Permission

Composition: Emi, G, C ▶

Use the Emi, G, and C chords to create your own song. Place the chords in the song chart below in any order you'd like. Then, pick one of the strumming patterns to play those chords.

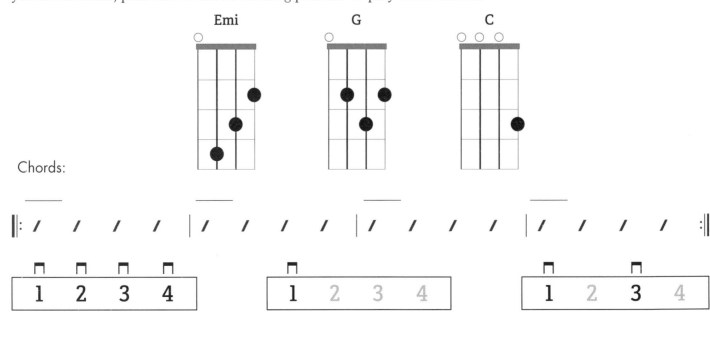

Chords: _____   _____   _____

‖: / / / / | / / / / | / / / / :‖

☐ ☐ ☐ ☐   ☐   ☐   ☐
1 2 3 4   **1** 2 3 4   **1** 2 **3** 4

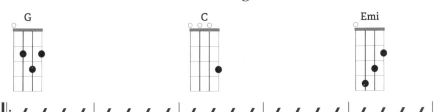

Full Band Song: I GOTTA FEELING
The Black Eyed Peas

Form of Recording: Intro–Chorus–Verse–Chorus–Verse–Chorus

Use this rhythm for the Chorus:

| 1 | 2 | 3 | 4 |

And use this rhythm for the Verse
(V means to strum up):

| 1 | + | 2 | + | 3 | + | 4 | + |

CHORUS
    G   **C**
I gotta feeling that tonight's gonna be a good night,

           Emi   **C**
That tonight's gonna be a good night, that tonight's gonna be a good, good night.

VERSE
G   **C**
Tonight's the night, let's live it up. I got my money, let's spend it up.

Emi   **C**
Go out and smash it, like, oh my God. Jump off that sofa, let's get, get off.

VERSE
G   **C**
I know that we'll have a ball if we get down and go out and just lose it all.

       Emi   **C**
I feel stressed out, I wanna let go. Let's go way out, spaced out, and losing all control.

VERSE
G   **C**
Fill up my cup, Mazel Tov! Look at her dancing, just take it off.

Emi
Let's paint the town, we'll shut it down.
    C
Let's burn the roof, and then we'll do it again.

Words and Music by Will Adams, Allan Pineda, Jaime Gomez, Stacy Ferguson, David Guetta and Frederic Riesterer
Copyright © 2009 BMG Sapphire Songs, I Am Composing LLC, BMG Platinum Songs US, Apl de Ap Publishing LLC,
Tab Magnetic Publishing, Headphone Junkie Publishing LLC, What A Publishing Ltd., KMR Music Royalties II SCSp,
Shapiro, Bernstein & Co. Inc. and Rister Editions
All Rights for BMG Sapphire Songs, I Am Composing LLC, BMG Platinum Songs US, Apl de Ap Publishing LLC,
Tab Magnetic Publishing and Headphone Junkie Publishing LLC Administered by BMG Rights Management (US) LLC
All Rights for What a Publishing Ltd. and KMR Music Royalties II SCSp Administered Worldwide by Kobalt Music Group Ltd.
All Rights for Shapiro, Bernstein & Co. Inc. and Rister Editions in the United States,
Ireland and the United Kingdom Administered by Reservoir Media Management, Inc.
All Rights Reserved   Used by Permission

Going Beyond: Singing and Playing
An important skill for a popular musician is to not only play songs, but also to sing along. Here are a few tips for singing and playing:

- Make sure you have learned the ukulele part well enough to play it without thinking about changing chords, then try speaking the lyrics in rhythm over it.
- Sing the lyrics while fretting the chords with just the left hand. Strum only when it's time to change chords.
- Don't worry too much about singing the correct pitches (notes) at this point; just practice the skill of doing two things at once.

SECTION 2

Playing Chords: One-Chord Song

Play the new chord A and use the strumming pattern below to play "Low Rider" by War. Make sure you strum down on the beats (⊓) and up on the "+" symbols (V).

LOW RIDER

War

You can also practice a different two-note solo over this song with the notes shown here:

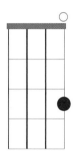

Music Theory: Reading Ukulele Tab

Tablature is another way to write music. It is used to write melodies and riffs. The ukulele tab **staff** has four lines, and each line represents a string. When the ukulele is in playing position, the string closest to your face is the lowest line on the tab staff.

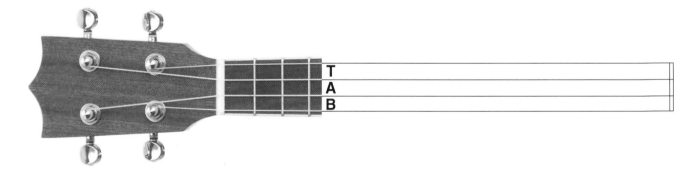

"Dark Horse" by Katy Perry has a riff played on the two strings closest to the ground: strings 1 and 2. The numbers on the lines tell us which fret to push down on which string. For now, listen to the original song to get a sense of the rhythm to play.

DARK HORSE
Katy Perry

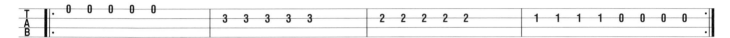

This next riff is also played on strings 1 and 2. The "0" in the tab means to play the string open, without pressing down any frets:

25 OR 6 TO 4
Chicago

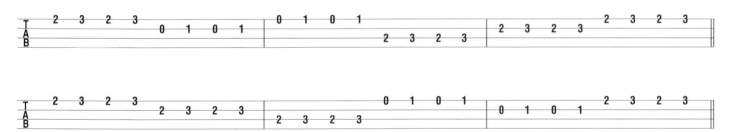

Instrument Technique: Strengthening Your Fingers

Tablature is also useful for notating exercises. Try the exercise below for moving between fingers 1 and 2. Repeat this exercise with different fingers and on different frets.

Playing Chords: Ami to C

Try switching between Ami and C with the song "Shout" by the Isley Brothers. Keep your fingers close to the strings to make switching between these chords simple and smooth.

SHOUT
The Isley Brothers

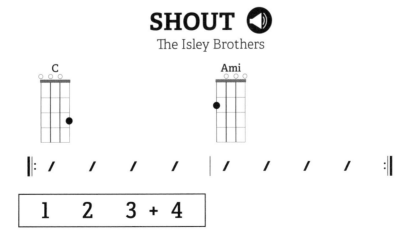

Playing Chords: E7

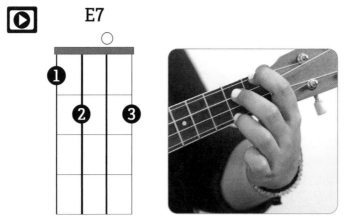

You can change between the E7 and C chords by shifting your ring finger from the 2nd fret to the 3rd fret on the 1st string while lifting your other fingers off the fretboard.

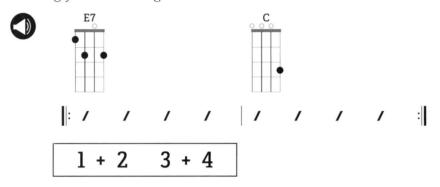

Improvisation: Four-Note Solo

You can expand the two-note solo to four notes by adding the open 2nd string and its 3rd-fret note. Try improvising your own melody using these four notes. Another musician can play the Ami chord along with you and the Jam Track.

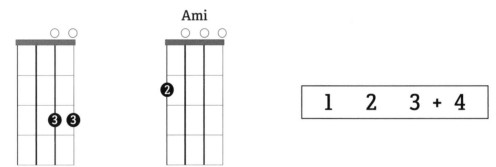

Music Theory: Whole Notes and Half Notes

In each measure of music so far, you have counted four beats. If you strum a chord once and let it ring for four beats, it lasts the whole measure. That is called a **whole note**. If it is cut in half, it becomes two **half notes**. Each whole note is four beats long and each half note is two beats long.

Below, whole and half notes in traditional notation are shown along with strumming notation.

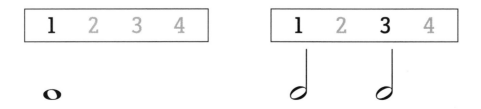

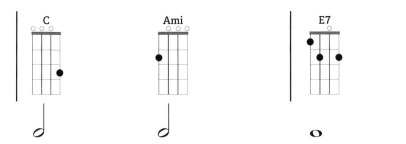

Full Band Song: HEATHENS

Twenty One Pilots

Form of Recording: Chorus–Verse–Chorus–Verse–Chorus–Chorus

Using traditional notation and chord diagrams, you can read and play the Chorus of "Heathens" by Twenty One Pilots.

Below is the full song shown with slashes and chord diagrams, as well as the chord and lyric chart. In addition to the full Jam Track for this song, there are also two separate Jam Tracks for the Chorus and Verse looped so you can practice them individually.

Notice that the Verse includes some different chords that you already know, but played on different beats than the Chorus pattern. The final B "chord" is something new.

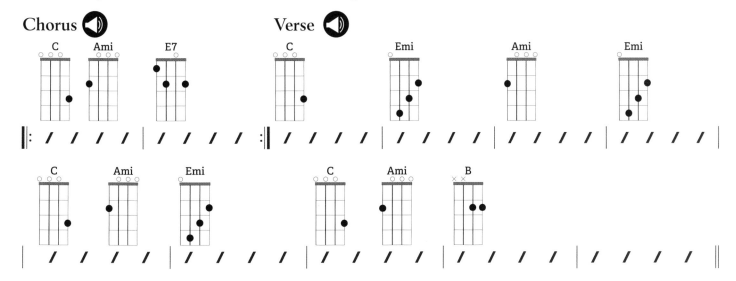

CHORUS

C   Ami   E7   C   Ami   E7
All my friends are heathens, take it slow. Wait for them to ask you who you know.

     C   Ami   E7   C   Ami   E7
Please don't make any sudden moves. You don't know the half of the abuse.

VERSE

C
Welcome to the room of people who have rooms of people
          Emi
     that they loved one day docked away.

Ami
Just because we check the guns at the door doesn't mean

       Emi
     our brains will change from hand grenades.

C   Ami   Emi
You'll never know the psychopath sitting next to you.
     You'll never know the murderer sitting next to you.

C   Ami   B
You'll think, "How'd I get here, sitting next to you?"
     But after all I've said, please don't forget.

SECTION 3

Instrument Technique: Chromatic Riffs

In this next tab example, use a different finger to play each different fret. When we move like this from one fret to the next in an upward or downward line, it is called **chromatic**. If you need to, you can move your hand up and down on the neck.

```
T
A    2        3        4        5       2        3        4        5       2        3        4        5
B
```

```
T    5     4     3     2              5     4     3     2
A
B                                                          5     4     3     2
```

Now, check out your chromatic skills with this heavy Led Zeppelin riff. Listen to the original recording to hear the rhythms.

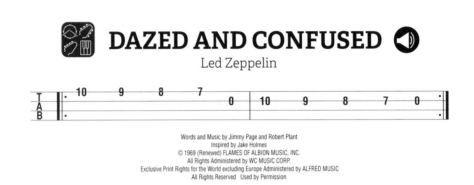

DAZED AND CONFUSED

Led Zeppelin

```
T    10   9   8   7                10   9    8    7
A                      0                            0
B
```

Playing Chords: D

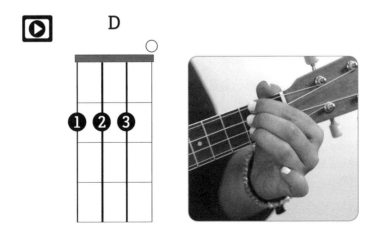

D

❶ ❷ ❸

Using the D and A chords, you can play a variety of songs.

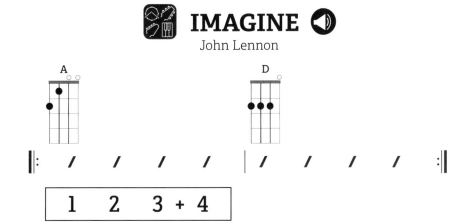

IMAGINE
John Lennon

```
1    2    3 + 4
```

A   **D**
Imagine no possessions.

A   **D**
I wonder if you can.

A   **D**
No need for greed or hunger,

A   **D**
A brotherhood of man.

BEST DAY OF MY LIFE
American Authors

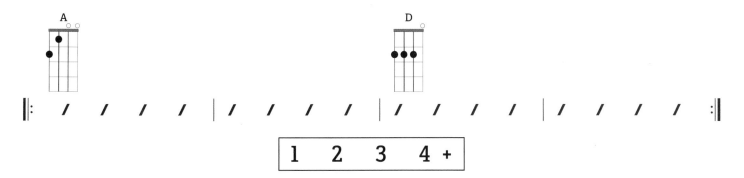

```
1    2    3    4 +
```

A
I had a dream so big and loud. I jumped so high I touched the clouds.

D
Whoa-o-o-o-o-oh. Whoa-o-o-o-o-oh.

A
I stretched my hands out to the sky. We danced with monsters through the night.

D
Whoa-o-o-o-o-oh. Whoa-o-o-o-o-oh.

A   **D**
Woo-o-o-o-oo! This is gonna be the best day of my life, my life.

A   **D**
Woo-o-o-o-oo! This is gonna be the best day of my life, my life.

Music Theory: Quarter and Eighth Notes

Half notes can be broken into two **quarter notes**. Each quarter note gets one beat.

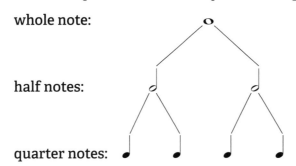

Playing and Resting

You can also use a **rest** when you want to stop the strings from ringing and leave some space. Try this with the A chord. A rest means "count, but don't play." Each **quarter rest** gets one beat.

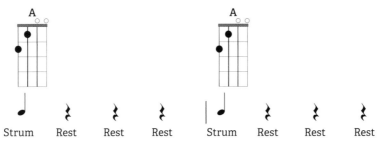

This strumming pattern is useful to practice changing chords.

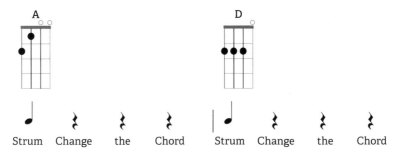

Quarter notes can be broken into **eighth notes**. Each eighth note gets a half of a beat.

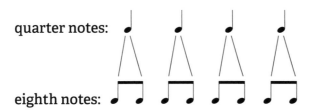

This rhythm:

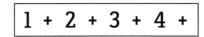

...is just eight eighth notes:

These strum patterns use quarter and eighth notes in different combinations. Try strumming and counting them.

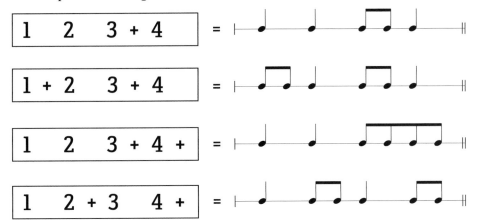

Improvisation: Six-Note Solo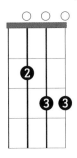

You can add two more notes to the four-note solo to make a six-note solo. The pattern of these notes creates what is called a pentatonic scale. You will learn more about pentatonic scales later in this book.

Composition: Compose a Riff

Using the notes in the six-note solo, create your own riff. Here are a few sample riffs:

Write your original riff here:

You can play your composed riff over the C to F chord progression. Here are some new strumming patterns you can use:

| 1 + 2 | 3 + 4 |

| 1 | 2 | 3 + 4 |

SECTION 4

Instrument Technique: Some New Riffs

Listen to the following songs to get a sense of the rhythms.

UNDER PRESSURE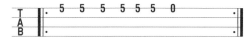
Queen ft. David Bowie

Practice this next riff using different finger combinations, or even just using your first finger the whole time.

SEVEN NATION ARMY
The White Stripes

Playing Chords: E

Next is the E major chord, which is your first **barre chord**. To play the E major chord, lay (or "bar") your first finger across all of the strings at the 4th fret. The barre is indicated in the chord diagram with a curved line, and the fret position is shown as "4th fr." Rock your finger back towards its side *ever so slightly* so that your finger remains flat and does not curve. Then use your pinky to depress the 7th fret of string 1. If this is too hard, you can remove the pinky and just play with your first finger across all of the strings for now.

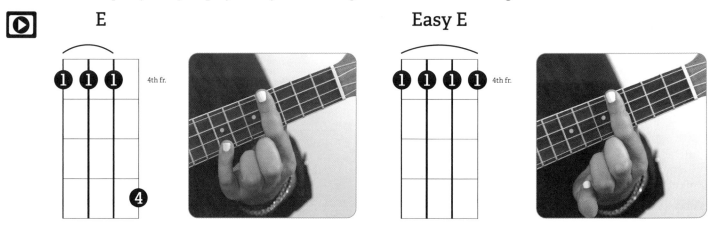

Try the E chord with this song:

WE WILL ROCK YOU
Queen

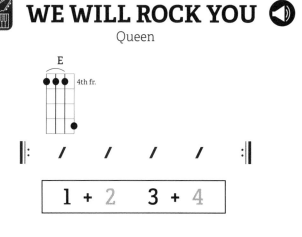

24

The next two songs have a variety of strum patterns to choose from. Some require you to play an up strum without playing a down strum. To do this, keep the up-and-down motion of your arm going, but just miss the strings on the way down. These patterns, in which upbeats are played after skipping downbeats, are called **syncopated** rhythms.

Notice that "Back in Black" includes the barre version of the D chord. It's exactly the same shape as the E barre chord you just learned but moved down two frets. This was done to make playing this song easier. You can also play the regular D chord shape if you like.

BACK IN BLACK

AC/DC

Here are several strum patterns you can use for this song, from most basic to most complex:

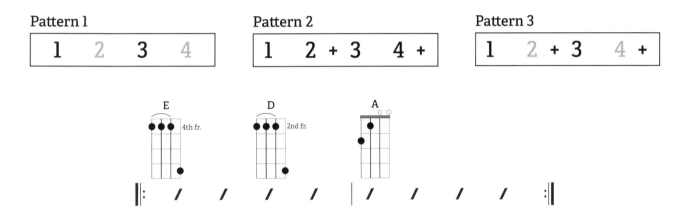

WHAT MAKES YOU BEAUTIFUL

One Direction

Here again are several strum patterns you can use for this song:

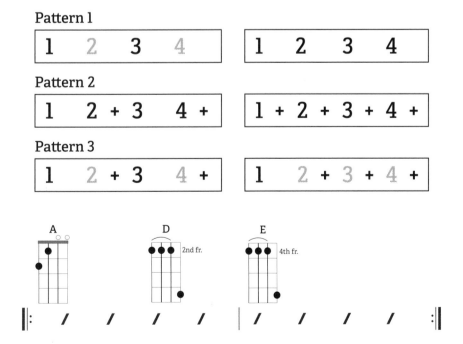

Composition: Writing Lyrics

Here are three steps you can take to write your own song lyrics:

1. Pick a theme. Lyrics can be easy to write when you have something you want to say. Think of something you care about and write based on that, such as friends, family, hobbies, or dreams.

2. Choose two words that rhyme, such as "great" and "late," or "thrill" and "chill." Then, choose another pair.

3. Turn your words into sentences. Try to speak the words in rhythm and sing them with the Jam Track. Here is an example of a verse for a song written about songwriting:

| Writing | lyrics | is | so | fun, | can | be | done | by | any - one. |

| / | / | / | / | | / | / | / | / |

| Think | of | what | to | write | a - bout; | play | some | chords, | and | sing | or | shout! |

| / | / | / | / | | / | / | / | / |

Full Band Song: STIR IT UP

Bob Marley & the Wailers

Form of Recording: Intro–Chorus–Verse–Chorus–Verse–Chorus

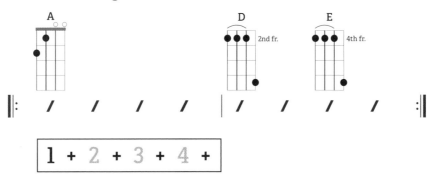

CHORUS

A   D   E   A   D   E

Stir it up. Little darlin', stir it up. Come on, baby.

          A   D   E   A   D   E

Come on and stir it up. Little darlin', stir it up. O-oh!

VERSE

   A   D

It's been a long, long time, yeah (stir it, stir it, stir it together).

E   A   D   E

Since I got you on my mind (ooh-ooh-ooh-ooh).

A   D   E

Now you are here (stir it, stir it, stir it together). I said, it's so clear.

  A   D   E

To see what we could do, baby (ooh-ooh-ooh-ooh). Just me and you.

Instrument Technique: Hammer-Ons 🔊 ▶️

To play a **hammer-on**, pluck the first note and then hammer your fret-hand fingertip down on the next note to create the sound without plucking it. Here are some examples. Try them with different finger combinations. In written music, the curved line above a hammer-on is called a **slur**, which tells you not to pluck the second note.

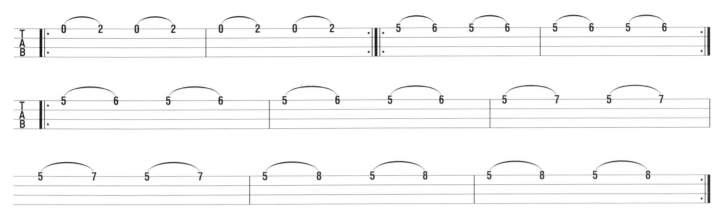

You can add hammer-ons into melodies you've already played:

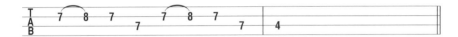

You can play that same melody on a different set of strings and frets.

You can also do multiple hammer-ons in a row, like in this song:

AM I EVIL? 🔊
Metallica

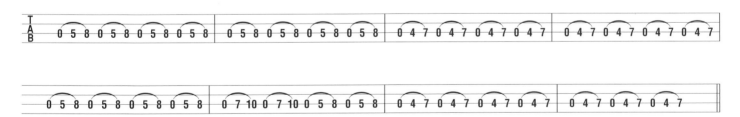

Music Theory: Notes, Chords, and Scales

All music is made up of the notes of the musical alphabet. All the riffs and chords you have been playing are made up of these individual notes. There are seven **natural notes**: A–B–C–D–E–F–G.

As you've already noticed, chords are a combination of notes played together.

A

Chord: multiple notes played together

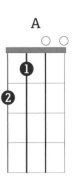

A **scale** is a series of notes. The notes we've been using for soloing are an example of a scale. Below is a sample scale that we will learn more about later in the book.

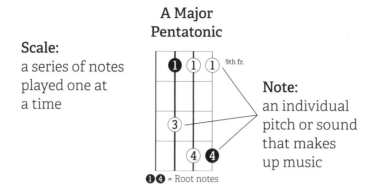

Scale:
a series of notes played one at a time

A Major Pentatonic

Note:
an individual pitch or sound that makes up music

= Root notes

The combination of notes, chords, and scales put to rhythm defines all the music we experience.

Instrument Technique: Fingerpicking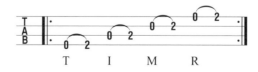

Up until now, we've been strumming all the notes of a chord at the same time. You can also pluck the notes of a chord separately, using your thumb (T), index (I), middle (M), and ring (R) fingers. When the notes of a chord are played separately, it is called an **arpeggio**. We'll assign one finger to each string for the exercises below:

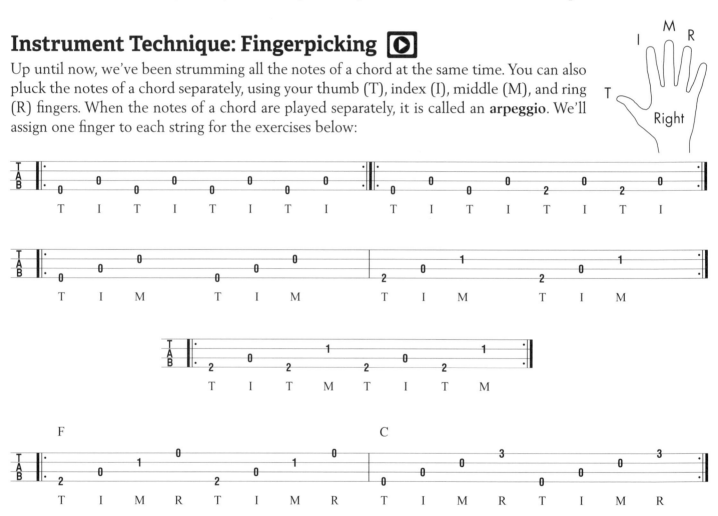

You can also use this technique to practice hammer-ons. Remember, assign your thumb to the 4th string, your index finger to the 3rd string, and so on.

The next fingerpicking riff uses the **pinch technique**, which is when you pluck two notes at the same time—one with your thumb and the other with one of your fingers. The fingering for the plucking hand is given, but you can experiment to see what feels comfortable for you.

HOME
Phillip Phillips

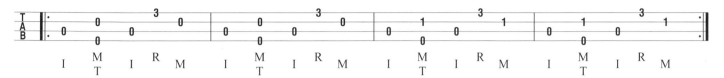

Improvisation: Minor Pentatonic Scale

The six-note solo you played earlier is called the **minor pentatonic scale**:

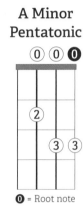

The **tonic**, or **root**, is the note a scale or chord is named after. For this scale, the tonic note is A, and it is the open 1st string. Remember, the darkened notes in scale diagrams indicate the root notes.

This scale sounds good with songs that have a bluesy or funky sound, like "Low Rider" by War.

One way to practice this scale is to play it using hammer-ons:

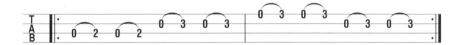

Here are a few riffs that use the pentatonic scale. Note the use of hammer-ons in a few measures.

Try to make some of your own riffs with the minor pentatonic scale:

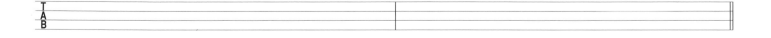

29

SECTION 6

Playing Chords: One-Chord Song

Here's a song that uses just one chord. You can practice with either a recording of the song or with your whole band.

 LAND OF A THOUSAND DANCES

Wilson Pickett

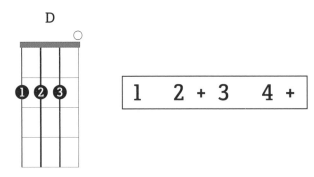

Instrument Technique: Pull-Offs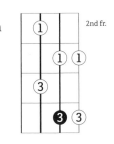

A **pull-off** is the opposite of a hammer-on. Instead of creating sound by hammering a finger down on the fretboard, create it by pulling a finger off. To get a full sound, you need to pull the finger downward off of the string, as opposed to just lifting it off.

Here are some riffs with pull-offs to open strings.

When pulling off to another fretted finger, be sure to hold the fretted finger in place. You can practice the technique with this new form of the A minor pentatonic scale:

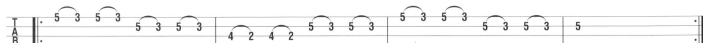

Improvisation: Applying Hammer-Ons and Pull-Offs

Try including hammer-ons and pull-offs in your improvisation. When using these techniques, make sure that the second note is as loud as the first. Here are some sample riffs.

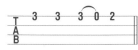 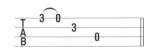  

Music Theory: The Music Staff

Look at this melody from a song you have already learned, "Heathens" by Twenty One Pilots. This is the vocal melody written in tablature:

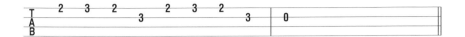

Every note on the ukulele has a place on the **music staff**. To start, look at a music staff, which is similar to a tab staff but with a few differences—there are five lines instead of four, and the lines *do not* refer to strings.

Ukulele Tablature		Standard Music Staff

vs.

The next important feature on a staff is the **treble clef**. It assigns specific note names to the lines and spaces on the staff.

You have already seen note heads used with rhythms. Here they are placed on the staff in the lines and spaces to let the musician know which notes to play. The vertical placement of each note determines what note it is. Here is the same vocal melody in both tab and staff notation.

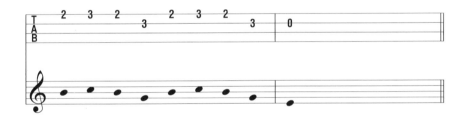

Finally, add the rhythms you learned earlier to the note heads on the staff. In the case of this song, there is a full measure of eighth notes followed by a whole note. Here, the eighth notes are beamed in groups of four instead of two.

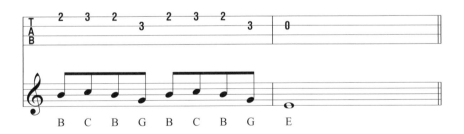

Each note is named by one of the seven (natural) letters of the musical alphabet. For now, look at the notes on the first three frets of the ukulele and on the first three strings. Notice that the staves are switched this time. In ukulele music, the tab staff is usually shown on the bottom.

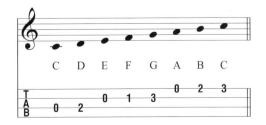

For the song below, write the notes of the tab numbers in the bottom staff for the first two measures. Then, write the tab numbers in the top staff for the notes shown in measures 3–5. We have slightly changed the rhythm so that it uses only the note values we have discussed so far.

BAD ROMANCE
Lady Gaga

Now, try playing your example, reading the staff notation and then the tab.

> From this point on, standard staff notation will be included with the tabs. Use this to begin familiarizing yourself with where the notes are on the staff. If you see any symbols or rhythms you don't understand, continue listening to the original recordings to hear the rhythms. You'll learn more about music reading as you continue through the Modern Band program.

To play the next melody from "Bad Romance," we'll need to know the **eighth rest**: ɣ. This rest takes the place of one eighth note. Combined with another eighth note or eighth rest, it makes up a full beat. Find a recording of this song and listen to the melody to hear how the rhythm works with the notation. This melody happens at the 0:29 mark on the original recording.

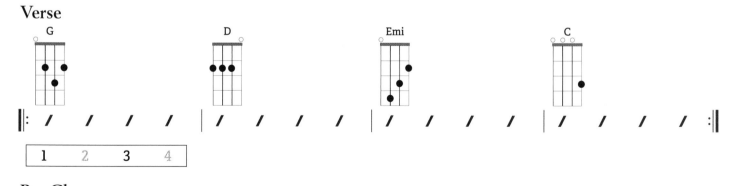

Full Band Song: SOMEONE LIKE YOU
Adele

Form of Recording: Intro–Verse–Pre-Chorus–Chorus–Verse–Pre-Chorus–Chorus–Bridge–Chorus

Verse

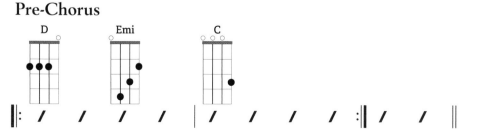

Pre-Chorus

Chorus

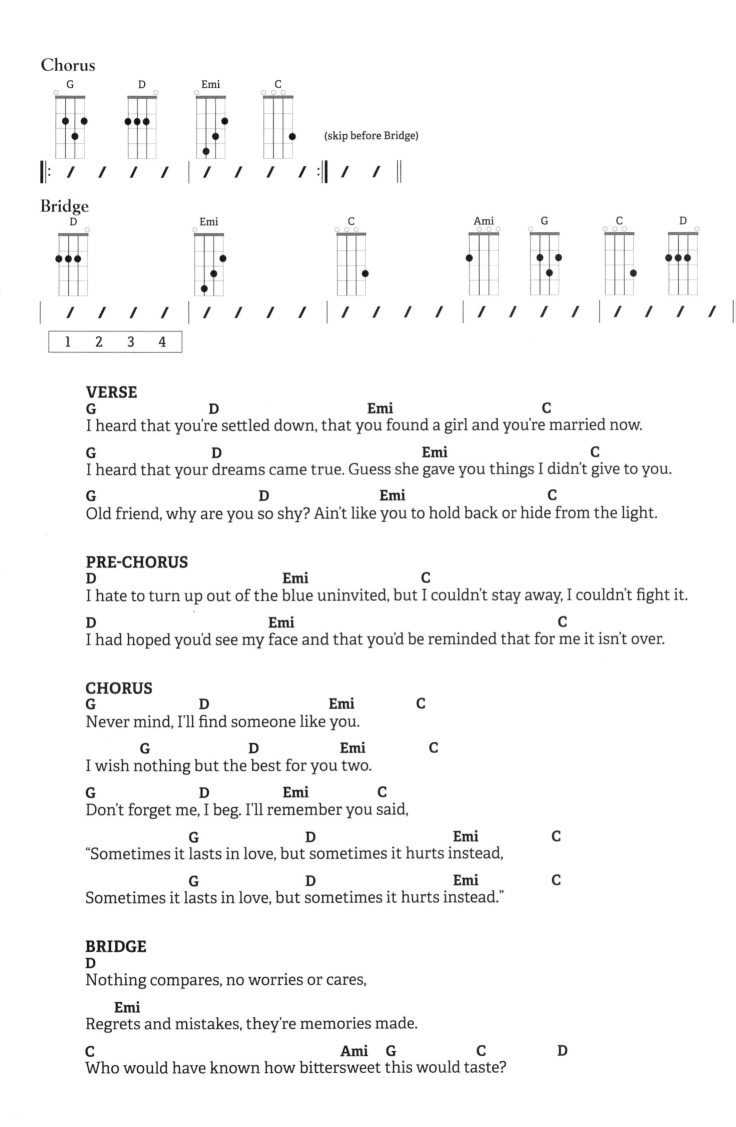

(skip before Bridge)

Bridge

| 1 | 2 | 3 | 4 |

VERSE

G   D   Emi   C
I heard that you're settled down, that you found a girl and you're married now.

G   D   Emi   C
I heard that your dreams came true. Guess she gave you things I didn't give to you.

G   D   Emi   C
Old friend, why are you so shy? Ain't like you to hold back or hide from the light.

PRE-CHORUS

D   Emi   C
I hate to turn up out of the blue uninvited, but I couldn't stay away, I couldn't fight it.

D   Emi   C
I had hoped you'd see my face and that you'd be reminded that for me it isn't over.

CHORUS

G   D   Emi   C
Never mind, I'll find someone like you.

         G   D   Emi   C
I wish nothing but the best for you two.

G   D   Emi   C
Don't forget me, I beg. I'll remember you said,

          G   D   Emi   C
"Sometimes it lasts in love, but sometimes it hurts instead,

          G   D   Emi   C
Sometimes it lasts in love, but sometimes it hurts instead."

BRIDGE

D
Nothing compares, no worries or cares,

      Emi
Regrets and mistakes, they're memories made.

C   Ami   G   C   D
Who would have known how bittersweet this would taste?

Playing Chords: Strumming Patterns

Practice playing through these patterns while staying on the same chord of your choice.

| 1 | 2 | 3 | 4 |

| 1 | 2 | 3 | 4 |

| 1 + 2 + 3 + 4 + |

| 1 | 2 + 3 + 4 + |

| 1 | 2 + 3 + 4 |

| 1 + 2 + 3 + 4 + |

Composition: Introduction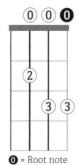

A lot of songs have an **introduction** (or intro). An introduction is often the instrumental section that happens before the vocalist begins. To compose an introduction, write four bars using the chords you know, and be sure to use at least one minor chord. Use the Jam Track to try out your ideas.

Chords:

_____   _____   _____   _____

‖: ╱ ╱ ╱ ╱ | ╱ ╱ ╱ ╱ | ╱ ╱ ╱ ╱ | ╱ ╱ ╱ ╱ :‖

Strumming Pattern:

Now add a riff to your introduction using this scale:

**A Minor
Pentatonic**

⓪ ⓪ **⓪**

②

③ ③

⓪ = Root note

T
A
B

Playing Chords: Major vs. Minor

Below, compare the sounds of the A and Ami chords, and the E and Emi chords. Each set of chords centers on the same pitch, but the two chords sound different. Notice the new chord shapes for E and Emi—more options for your growing chord vocabulary!

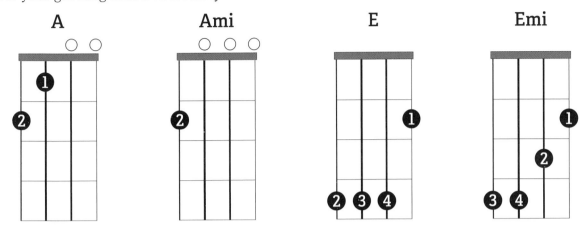

Play the following two progressions and pay attention to the difference in sound. You can select the strum pattern:

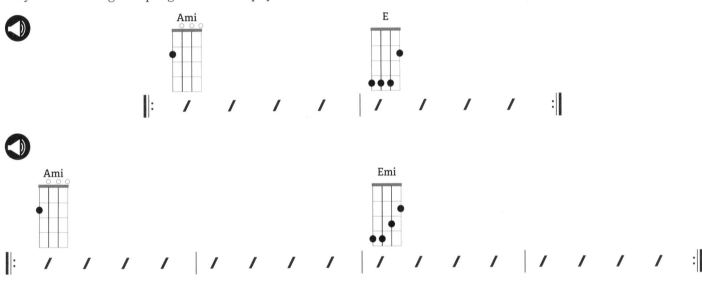

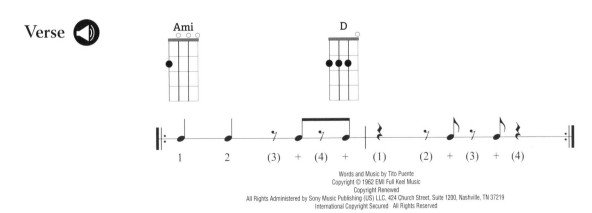

Here's the breakdown that happens periodically throughout the song. It happens first at the 30-second mark. On the Jam Track, the main riff is played four times through before the breakdown comes in.

Breakdown 1

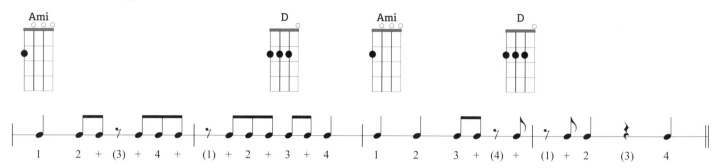

Here's one more section, which is played over an E chord. As before, the main riff alternates with this section on the Jam Track.

Breakdown 2

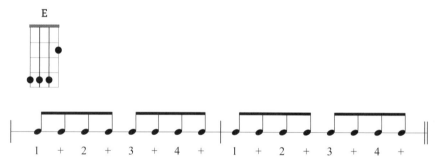

VERSE

Ami   **D**
Oye como va, mi ritmo.

Ami   **D**
Bueno pa gozar, mulata.

Ami   **D**
Oye como va, mi ritmo.

Ami   **D**
Bueno pa gozar, mulata.

SECTION 8

Instrument Technique: Riffs

One way to keep your fingers nimble is to learn more riffs. Here are a couple of riffs that focus on strings 1 and 2.

COME AS YOU ARE 🔊

Nirvana

U CAN'T TOUCH THIS 🔊

MC Hammer

UPTOWN FUNK 🔊

Mark Ronson ft. Bruno Mars

Instrument Technique: Chucking and Selective Muting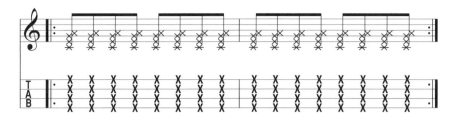

Place the fingers of your fretting hand gently against the strings, so that you're touching them but not pressing them down. Then, strum the strings to create a percussive, muted sound. This technique is called **chucking**. In written music, muted strings and chucks are indicated with "X" noteheads.

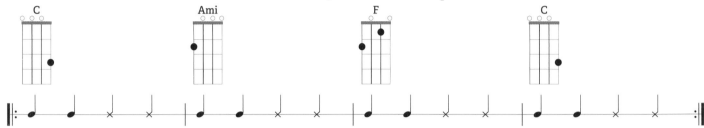

You can also alternate between chords and chucks, like in this example:

To **selectively mute** strings, use available fingers on the fret hand to gently touch the strings that you want to stop from ringing out. For example, play the C chord but lightly touch strings 4, 3, and 2 with your first and second fingers to mute the strings, like in the photo:

Now, try this technique with a song. The strumming pattern for the introduction of "House of Gold" uses sixteenth notes (♪ or ♫). Sixteenth notes last for a quarter of a beat each, and the way you count them is "1 e & a, 2 e & a, 3 e & a, 4 e & a."

Remember, muted strings are indicated with an "X" on the tab and standard notation staves.

HOUSE OF GOLD
Twenty One Pilots

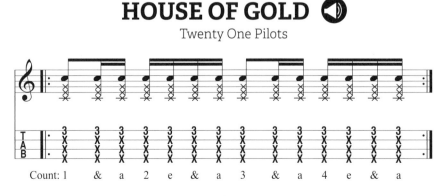

Words and Music by Tyler Joseph
© 2013 WARNER-TAMERLANE PUBLISHING CORP. and STRYKER JOSEPH MUSIC
All Rights Administered by WARNER-TAMERLANE PUBLISHING CORP.
All Rights Reserved   Used by Permission

Instrument Technique: Syncopation and Muted Strums

Earlier, you played various syncopated strumming patterns. A common technique to add to these strumming patterns is the percussive muted string strum.

To get this sound, drop your palm to the strings as you strum so that they don't have a chance to ring out.

Then, without lifting your hand off the strings, strum through these muted strings. The strings should click, rather than ring out.

For this next song, mute the strings on beat 2. Then, lift your palm off the strings before you play the upstroke on the "and" of beat 2. Practice this slowly until you can play the muted strum in one continuous motion. Try it out first with just the Emi chord:

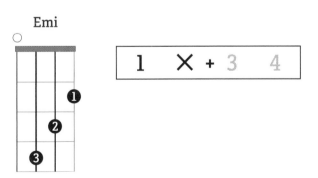

Now, try this technique with a song:

HELLO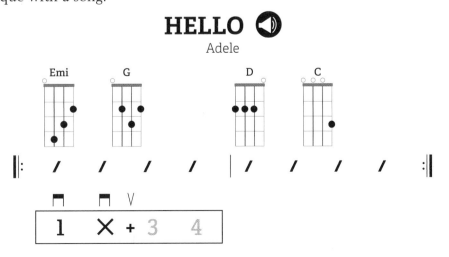
Adele

39

Use the same strumming pattern on this next song:

SEE YOU AGAIN

Wiz Khalifa ft. Charlie Puth

Try applying muted strumming to a song you played earlier using this syncopated reggae pattern. Because of the slow tempo of this song, all of the strums will be down strums:

STIR IT UP

Bob Marley & the Wailers

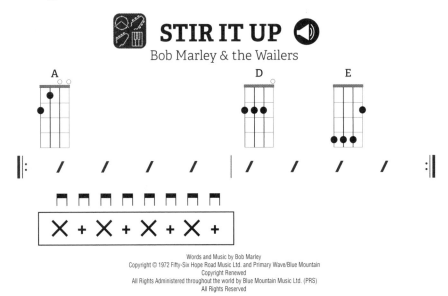

Here's another song that uses the muted strum. We're using sixteenth notes again, and we're muting the chords on the downbeats of 2 and 4.

OVER THE RAINBOW

Israel Kamakawiwoʻole

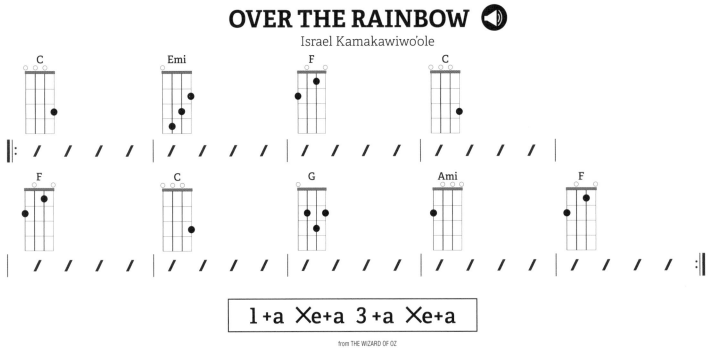

Full Band Song: WAKA WAKA (THIS TIME FOR AFRICA)

Shakira

Form of Recording: Intro–Verse–Pre-Chorus–Chorus–Interlude–Verse– Pre-Chorus–Chorus–Bridge–Chorus

For this song, you will play the same chords for each section.

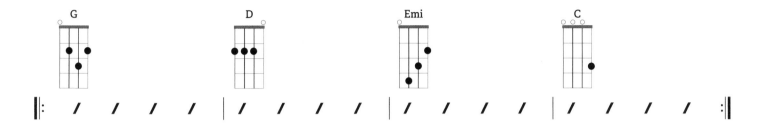

However, how you play those chords can vary from section to section. For the Verse, strum whole notes:

During the Chorus, you can emphasize the kick and snare drum pattern by plucking just the root notes of the chord before playing the full chord.

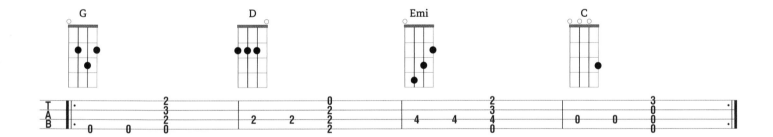

The Official 2010 FIFA World Cup Song
Words and Music by Shakira, Zolani Mahola, John Hill, Eugene Victor Doo Belley, Jean Ze Bella and Emile Kojidie
Copyright © 2010 Sony Music Publishing (US) LLC, MyMPM Music, Freshly Ground, EMI April Music Inc., RodeoMan Music and Sony Music Publishing (Germany) Gmbh
All Rights Administered by Sony Music Publishing (US) LLC, 424 Church Street, Suite 1200, Nashville, TN 37219
International Copyright Secured   All Rights Reserved

Going Beyond: Sixteenth Notes

During the Pre-Chorus of "Waka Waka," try the ukulele strumming pattern using sixteenth notes. Use your ear to hear the snare drum hits on the recording, which are played in the same rhythm. Be sure to play these notes short by muting the strings right after you play them.

VERSE

G   D
You're a good soldier, choosing your battles.

    Emi   C
    Pick yourself up and dust yourself off and get back in the saddle.

G   D
You're on the front line, everyone's watching.

    Emi   C
    You know it's serious, we're getting closer, this isn't over.

G   D   Emi   C
The pressure's on, you feel it. But you got it all, believe it.

PRE-CHORUS

G   D
When you fall get up, oh, oh. And if you fall get up, eh, eh.

    Emi   C
    Tsamina mina zangalewa, 'cause this is Africa.

CHORUS

G   D   Emi   C
Tsamina mina, eh, eh. Waka waka, eh, eh. Tsamina mina zangalewa, this time for Africa.

VERSE

G   D   Emi
Listen to your God. This is our motto. Your time to shine,

               C
    don't wait in line, y vamos por todo.

G   D   Emi
People are raising their expectations. Go on and feed them,

               C
    this is your moment, no hesitation.

G   D   Emi   C
Today's your day, I feel it. You paved the way, believe it.

PRE-CHORUS

G   D
If you get down get up, oh, oh. When you get down get up, eh, eh.

    Emi   C
    Tsamina mina zangalewa, this time for Africa.

BRIDGE

G
Awabuye lamajoni, ipikipiki mama wa A to Z.

Bathi susa lamajoni, ipikipiki mama from East to West.

Bathi waka waka ma eh eh, waka waka ma eh eh,

Zonk' izizwe mazibuye, 'cause this is Africa.

SECTION 9

Music Theory: Transcribing Notation

The first four measures of the next song are written in tab. Play through the melody, then write in the correct pitches on the traditional staff. The first note is provided for you.

LITTLE TALKS
Of Monsters and Men

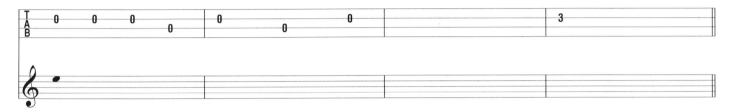

The last four measures are written below in staff notation. Write in the tab numbers. Don't worry about the rhythmic notation for now.

This last example has **dots** and **ties**. When you see a dotted note, the dot adds half the value of the note to itself. So, a **dotted quarter note** is one and a half beats.

Remember, ties connect notes. For example, the tied quarter and whole notes equal a total of five beats. You pick only the first note and then let it ring for five beats.

Playing Chords: More Great Songs

The following songs use all the chords you've learned so far.

HEY THERE DELILAH
Plain White T's

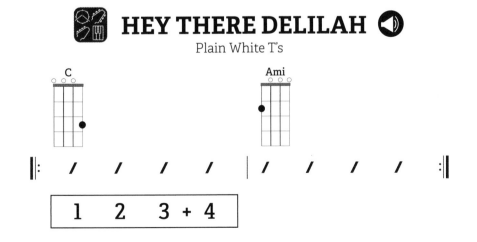

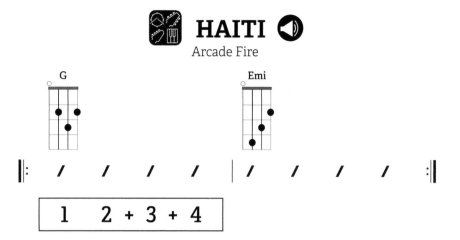

HAITI
Arcade Fire

On this next song, play G on beats 1 and 2, then switch to C and play it on the "and" of beat 3 and again on beat 4. In the second measure, play the same pattern but this time with the D and C chords.

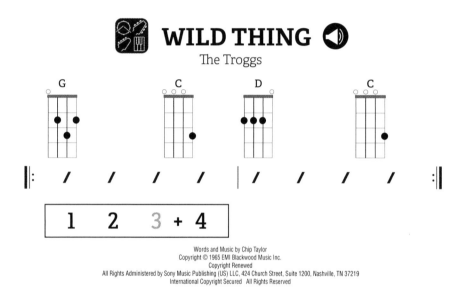

WILD THING
The Troggs

Below is one of the most popular chord progressions in all of popular music:

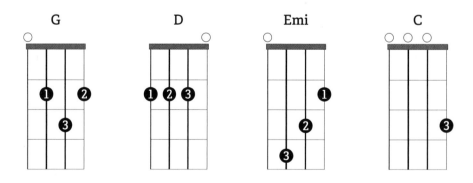

This progression can be found in many songs from the last 60 years, including "Where Is the Love," "Bored to Death," "Demons," "Apologize," "The Edge of Glory," "Someone Like You," and hundreds of others. Try it with the Chorus of the pop song "The Edge of Glory" by Lady Gaga.

THE EDGE OF GLORY

Lady Gaga

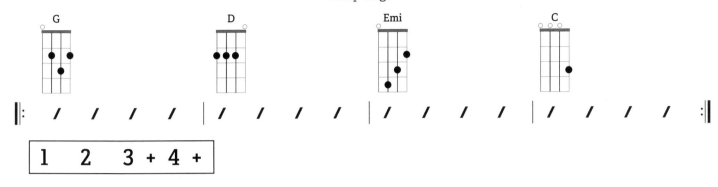

```
1   2   3 + 4 +
```

      G   D   Emi   C
I'm on the edge of glory, and I'm hanging on a moment of truth.

      G   D   Emi   C
Out on the edge of glory, and I'm hanging on a moment with you.

      G   D   Emi   C
I'm on the edge, the edge, the edge, the edge, the edge, the edge, the edge.

      G   D   Emi   C
I'm on the edge of glory, and I'm hanging on a moment with you.

                 G
I'm on the edge with you.

Composition: Verse and Chorus

Now, let's use chords to compose songs. Create a new four-chord verse and chorus, using any of the seven chords you have already learned (A, Ami, C, D, E, Emi, and G). Try using a syncopated rhythm for either your verse or chorus.

Verse Chords:

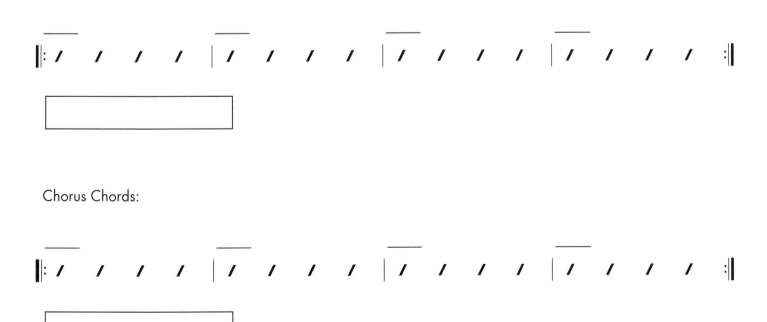

Chorus Chords:

Improvisation: Major Pentatonic Scale

The **major pentatonic scale** looks a lot like the minor pentatonic scale. The only difference between the two scales is which note feels like home, or the **tonic**. Here are a couple sample riffs you can play over the Jam Track.

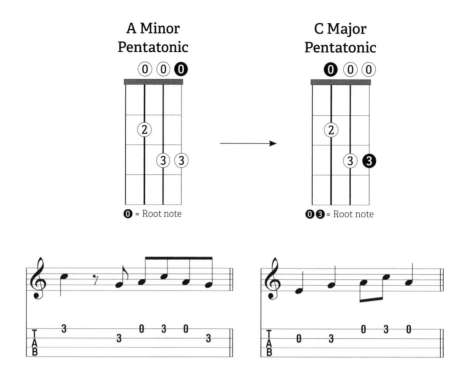

Try the scale over a few familiar progressions, this time at the 9th fret.

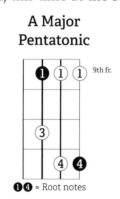

WAITING IN VAIN
Bob Marley & the Wailers

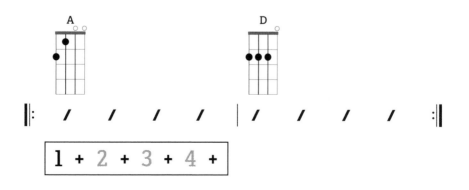

The scale pattern for this next song has the same shape but is moved down two frets.

G Major
Pentatonic

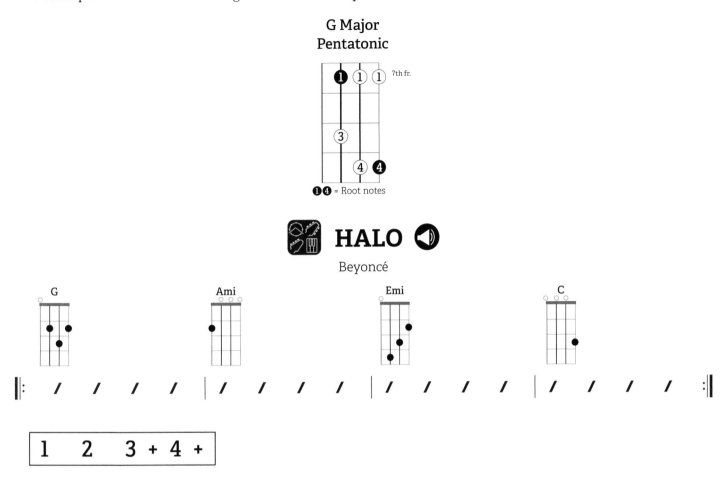

● ❹ = Root notes

HALO 🔊

Beyoncé

| G | Ami | Emi | C |

| 1 | 2 | 3 | + | 4 | + |

Full Band Song: BEST DAY OF MY LIFE 🔊

American Authors

Form of Recording: Intro–Verse–Pre-Chorus–Chorus–Verse–Pre-Chorus–Chorus–Bridge–Chorus

This song combines several of the skills you have learned so far: chords, riffs, and a solo. In the fourth bar of the Pre-Chorus, there is a measure with no chord. Don't play during that measure of music.

Verse/Chorus 🔊

| D | | | G |

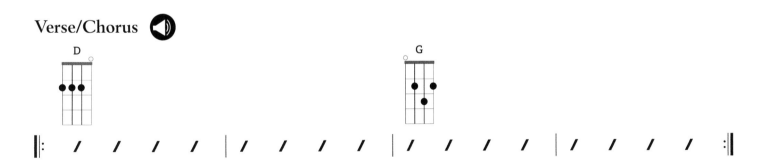

Pre-Chorus

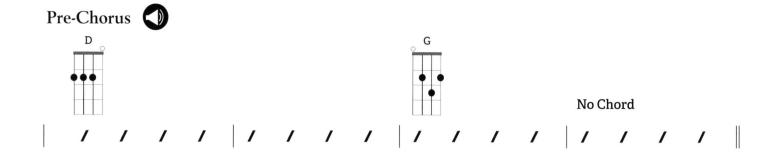

No Chord

Bridge

Chorus Riff

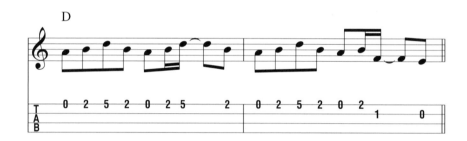

This song has ukulele riffs in the intro and chorus (the Chorus Riff you just learned). You can also use the D major pentatonic scale to create your own solo. Use the D major pentatonic scale because the song is in the **key** of D major.

**D Major
Pentatonic**

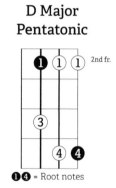

● ❹ = Root notes

VERSE

D
I had a dream so big and loud. I jumped so high I touched the clouds.

G
Whoa-o-o-o-o-oh. Whoa-o-o-o-o-oh.

D
I stretched my hands out to the sky. We danced with monsters through the night.

G
Whoa-o-o-o-o-oh. Whoa-o-o-o-o-oh.

PRE-CHORUS

D   **Emi**
I'm never gonna look back, whoa. I'm never gonna give it up, no. Please don't wake me now.

CHORUS

D   **G**
Wo-o-o-o-oo! This is gonna be the best day of my life, my life.

D   **G**
Wo-o-o-o-oo! This is gonna be the best day of my life, my life.

VERSE

D
I howled at the moon with friends. And then the sun came crashing in.

G
Whoa-o-o-o-o-oh. Whoa-o-o-o-o-oh.

      D
But all the possibilities, no limits just epiphanies.

G
Whoa-o-o-o-o-oh. Whoa-o-o-o-o-oh.

BRIDGE

D
I hear it calling outside my window.

I feel it in my soul, soul.

The stars were burning so bright,

The sun was out 'til midnight.

I say we lose control, control.

SECTION 10

Instrument Technique: Pentatonic Riffs

Here are a few more pentatonic riffs so you can see the scale in action.

LOVE ON THE WEEKEND
John Mayer

This next riff is played with a **shuffle feel**. This means the eighth notes are played in an uneven rhythm. You've probably heard this popular sound before in countless blues, rock, pop, and jazz songs. Listen to the original recording of this classic blues riff and play with the Jam Track to get a feel for it.

MANNISH BOY
Muddy Waters

Music Theory: Tab vs. Notation

Check out the pentatonic riff from the song below. In the first example, try playing it using just staff notation.

CLOSER
The Chainsmokers ft. Halsey

One of the cool things about ukulele and notation is that you can play the same notes in multiple places on the fretboard. Here is the same riff in tab. As you can see, there is more than one way to play the notes in the standard notation.

The sound quality will change depending on where you choose to play this melody. You can try different ways and listen for which you like best.

Instrument Technique: Chord Variations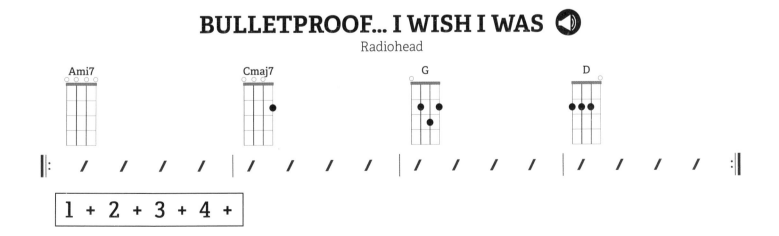

You can modify the sound of your chords by making slight changes to the notes.

C becomes Cmaj7 ("C major seven") by playing the 2nd fret instead of the 3rd.

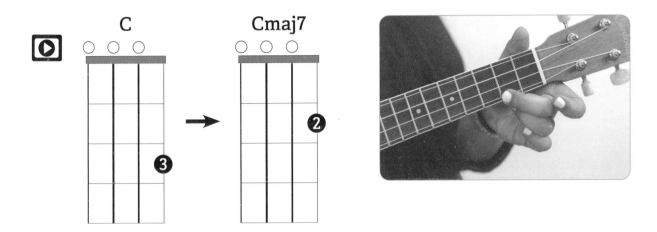

Ami becomes an Ami7 ("A minor seven") when you remove your middle finger and play all four strings open.

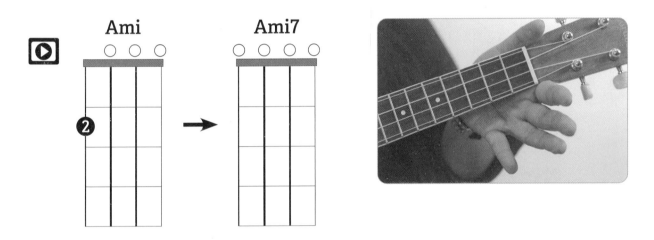

Try switching between them using this song's chord progression:

BULLETPROOF... I WISH I WAS
Radiohead

Ami7   Cmaj7   G   D

‖: / / / / | / / / / | / / / / | / / / / :‖

1 + 2 + 3 + 4 +

These are just a couple of examples of chords you can create with small alterations. Spend some time making slight changes to the chords you already know to hear how they sound. Here are a few more examples using the D chord:

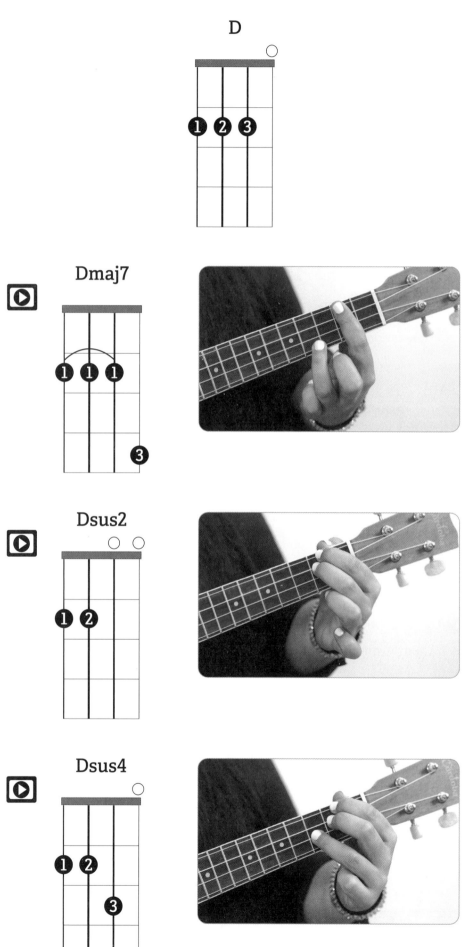

D

Dmaj7

Dsus2

Dsus4

And here is a variation on the F chord:

Fmaj7

Several of these chords will be used in the next Full Band Song.

Playing Chords: Dmi

Dmi

Here is a song that uses Dmi:

UPTOWN FUNK 🔊
Mark Ronson ft. Bruno Mars

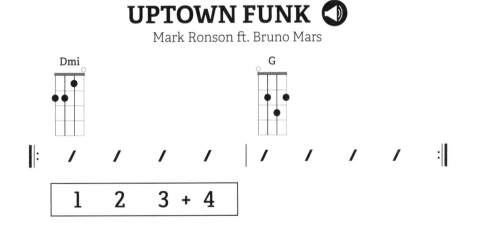

Dmi   G

‖: / / / / | / / / / :‖

1   2   3 + 4

Full Band Song: KICK, PUSH

Lupe Fiasco

Form of Recording: Verse–Chorus–Verse–Chorus–Verse–Chorus

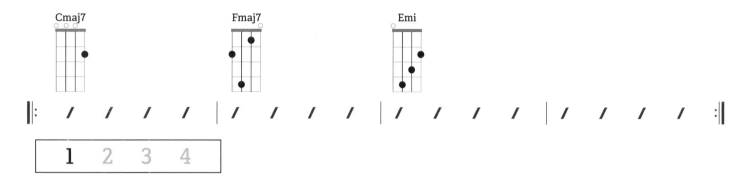

Verse/Chorus Riff

VERSE

First got it when he was six, didn't know any tricks. Matter fact,

First time he got on it he slipped, landed on his hip and bust his lip.

For a week he had to talk with a lisp, like this.

Now we can end the story right here,

But shorty didn't quit, it was something in the air, yea.

He said it was somethin' so appealing. He couldn't fight the feelin'.

Somethin' about it, he knew he couldn't doubt it, couldn't understand it,

Brand it, since the first kickflip he landed, uh. Labeled a misfit, abandoned,

Ca-kunk, ca-kunk, kunk. His neighbors couldn't stand it, so he was banished to the park.

Started in the morning, wouldn't stop till after dark, yea.

When they said "it's getting late in here, so I'm sorry young man, there's no skating here."

CHORUS

So we kick, push, kick, push, kick, push, kick, push, coast.

And the way he roll just a rebel to the world with no place to go.

So we kick, push, kick, push, kick, push, kick, push, coast.

So come and skate with me, just a rebel looking for a place to be.

So let's kick, and push, and coast.

VERSE

Uh, uh, uh. My man got a lil' older, became a better roller (yea).

No helmet, hell-bent on killin' himself, was what his momma said.

But he was feelin' himself, got a lil' more swagger in his style.

Met his girlfriend, she was clappin' in the crowd.

Love is what was happening to him now, uh. He said "I would marry you but I'm engaged to

These aerials and varials, and I don't think this board is strong enough to carry two."

She said "beau, I weigh 120 pounds. Now, lemme make one thing clear, I don't need to ride

yours, I got mine right here." So she took him to a spot he didn't know about,

Somewhere in the apartment parking lot, she said, "I don't normally take dates in here."

Security came and said, "I'm sorry there's no skating here."

CHORUS

So they kick, push, kick, push, kick, push, kick, push, coast.

And the way they roll, just lovers intertwined with no place to go.

And so they kick, push, kick, push, kick, push, kick, push, coast.

So come and skate with me, just a rebel looking for a place to be.

So let's kick, and push, and coast.

VERSE

Yea uh, yea, yea. Before he knew he had a crew that wasn't no punk

In they Spitfire shirts and SB Dunks. They would push, till they couldn't skate no more.

Office buildings, lobbies wasn't safe no more.

And it wasn't like they wasn't getting chased no more,

Just the freedom is better than breathing, they said.

An escape route, they used to escape out when things got crazy they needed to break out.

(They'd head) to any place with stairs, and good grinds the world was theirs, uh.

And they four wheels would take them there,

Until the cops came and said, "There's no skating here."

CHORUS

So they kick, push, kick, push, kick, push, kick, push, coast.

And the way they roll, just rebels without a cause with no place to go.

And so they kick, push, kick, push, kick, push, kick, push, coast.

So come roll with me, just a rebel looking for a place to be.

So let's kick, and push, and coast.

SECTION 11

Music Theory: Blues Scale

Both of these riffs use the **blues scale**. You can use this scale to write riffs or play solos. The blues scale is similar to the minor pentatonic scale with an added "blue" note. Remember to start on string 3 to play scales from the lowest notes to the highest notes due to how ukuleles are tuned. Here it is in C:

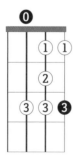

Try writing a riff using notes in the blues scale:

Instrument Technique: Slides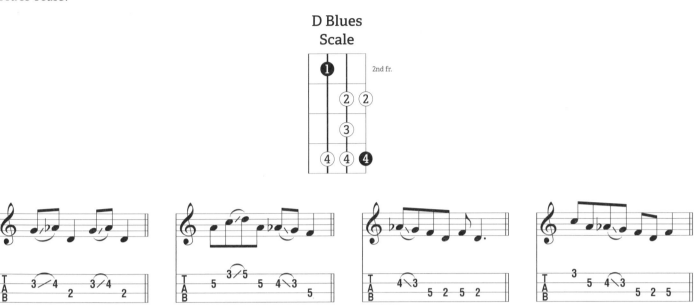

There are several different types of **slides** you can play on the ukulele. We will focus on a common slide that moves from one note to another on the same string without lifting off the fretboard. Similar to hammer-ons and pull-offs, the slur in the notation tells you not to pick the second note. Try these examples using the D blues scale:

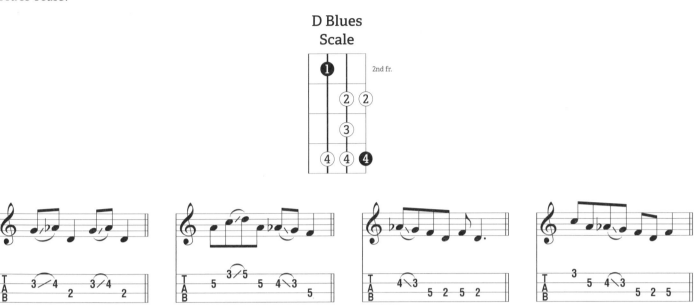

Play a solo over the next song using the D blues scale and add some slides to it, along with hammer-ons and pull-offs. If you find something cool, write in the tab below!

EVIL WAYS
Santana

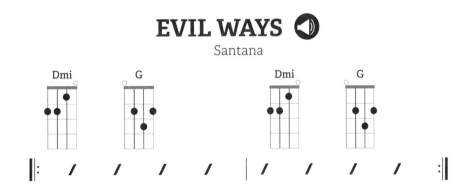

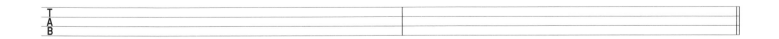

Instrument Technique: Power Chords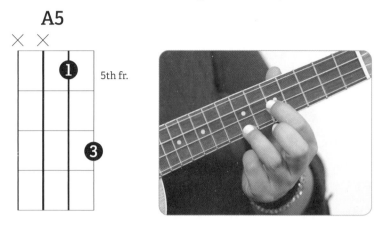

Power chords will allow you to play even more songs. Power chords have simple shapes that can be easily moved up or down the fretboard. Start with a two-note power chord, A5:

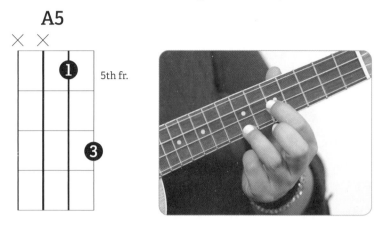

Just move your hand shape up and down the fretboard to change chords. Try it on the next song.

STRAY CAT STRUT

Stray Cats

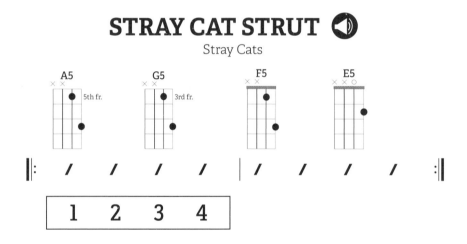

Power chords can be played on the 2nd and 3rd strings as well:

You can also play three-note power chords using a barre. In this case, you can lay your ring or pinky finger flat across the two higher notes in the chord, pressing them both down with the finger that feels most comfortable for you.

A5

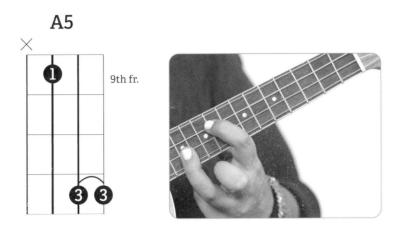

9th fr.

Here is a song that uses power chords on both the 1st and 2nd strings and the 2nd and 3rd strings:

SMELLS LIKE TEEN SPIRIT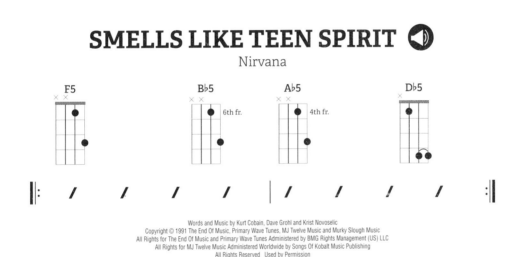
Nirvana

Composition: Composing with Power Chords

To write a song with power chords, choose a fret number between 1 and 10. Play a power chord at that location with your first finger on the 2nd string and your ring finger on the 1st string, two frets higher. Pick four chords this way and write a rhythm to play them with.

Full Band Song: UMBRELLA

Rihanna

Form of Recording: Intro–Verse–Chorus–Verse–Chorus–Bridge–Chorus

For this song, you can play this riff in the Intro and first Verse:

Intro/Verse

Here are the chords for the Verse:

Verse

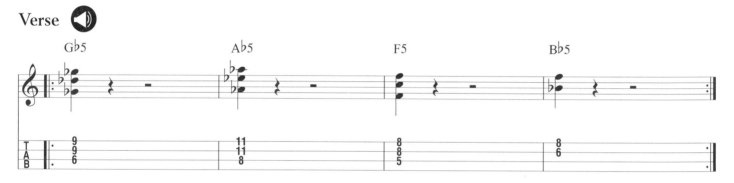

In the Chorus section, you can play sustained power chords. Notice the different fingering for Db5. It's an **inversion**, with the root note, Db, on the top instead of the bottom.

Chorus

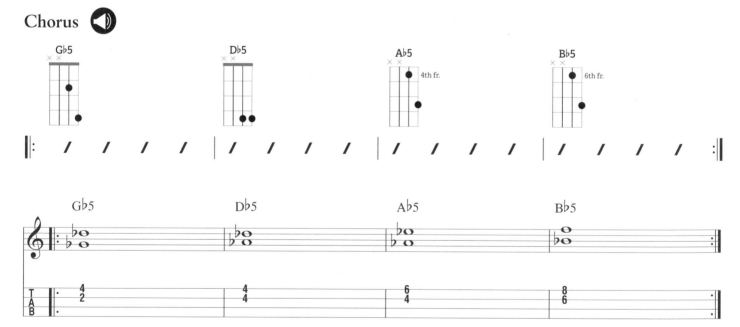

Often in music, material is repeated but with different endings. To show this, we can write **first and second endings** in the notation. These are the measures under the brackets labeled "1." and "2." To play this, perform the first four measures of Verse 2 below and then repeat. When playing it the second time, skip the first ending and play the second ending.

Verse 2

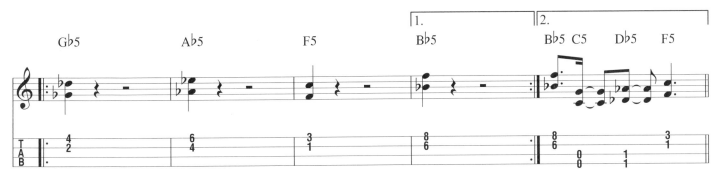

You can also play power chords in the Bridge, which has a first and second ending as well. Play the four measures before the repeat sign the first time, then skip the first ending the second time and jump to the second ending.

Bridge

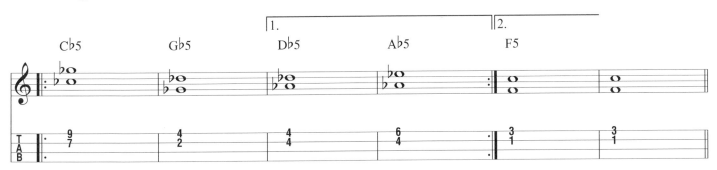

You can use the B♭ blues scale to solo over all the sections except the Bridge.

**B♭ Blues
Scale**

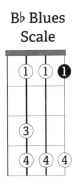

VERSE

    G♭5   **A♭5**
You have my heart, and we'll never be worlds apart.

             F5   **B♭5**
Maybe in magazines, but you'll still be my star.

             G♭5   **A♭5**
Baby, 'cause in the dark you can't see shiny cars.

                  F5   **B♭5**
And that's when you need me there, with you I'll always share, because...

CHORUS

G♭5   **D♭5**   **A♭5**
When the sun shines, we'll shine together. Told you I'd be here forever.

                      B♭5
Said I'll always be your friend. Took an oath, I'mma stick it out 'til the end.

G♭5   **D♭5**   **A♭5**
Now that it's raining more than ever, know that we'll still have each other.

                      B♭5   **G♭5**
You can stand under my umbrella. You can stand under my umbrella.

         D♭5   **A♭5**
(Ella, ella, eh, eh, eh.) Under my umbrella.

         B♭5   **G♭5**
(Ella, ella, eh, eh, eh.) Under my umbrella.

         D♭5   **A♭5**
(Ella, ella, eh, eh, eh.) Under my umbrella.

         B♭5
(Ella, ella, eh, eh, eh, eh, eh, eh.)

VERSE

    G♭5   **A♭5**
These fancy things, will never come in between.

                 F5   **B♭5**
You're part of my entity, here for infinity.

                G♭5   **A♭5**
When the war has took its part, when the world has dealt its cards,

    F5   **B♭5**
If the hand is hard, together we'll mend your heart.

BRIDGE

C♭5   **G♭5**
You can run into my arms. It's OK, don't be alarmed.

         D♭5   **A♭5**
Come here to me. There's no distance in between our love.

C♭5   **G♭5**
So go on and let the rain pour.

                    F5
I'll be all you need and more, because...

SECTION 12

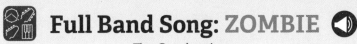

Full Band Song: ZOMBIE
The Cranberries

Form of Recording: Intro–Verse–Chorus–Verse–Chorus–Bridge–Chorus–Outro

This last song combines several of the elements you've learned in this book:

- Standard chords
- Power chords
- Chord variations
- Tab reading
- Hammer-ons
- Pull-offs

Here is the whole song. Choose your own strum patterns for the different sections. For the Chorus, though, follow the tab part for the power chords.

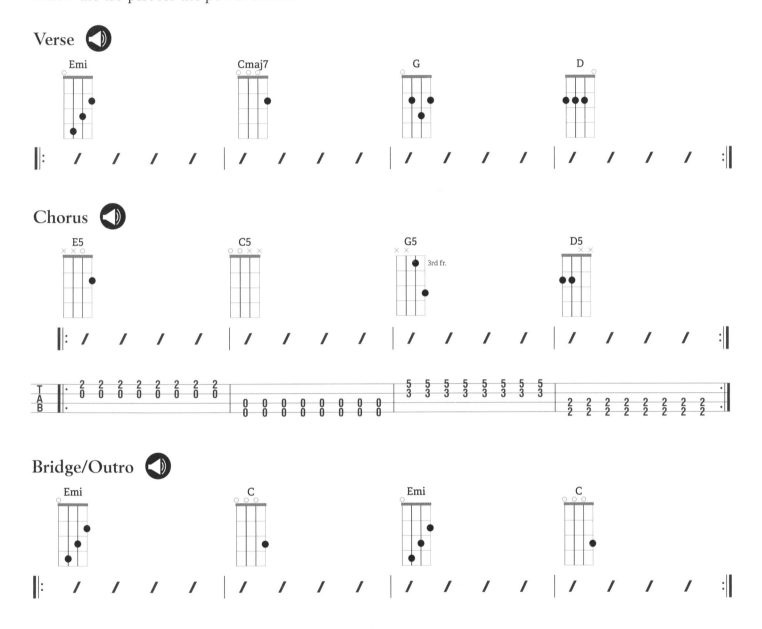

Here is the ukulele riff at the end of the Chorus:

Here is the ukulele riff played during the Outro:

VERSE

Emi   Cmaj7   G   D
Another head hangs lowly, child is slowly taken.

Emi   Cmaj7   G   D
And the violence caused such silence. Who are we mistaken?

       Emi   Cmaj7   G   D
But you see it's not me, it's not my family. In your head, in your head they are fighting,

          Emi   Cmaj7
With their tanks, and their bombs, and their bombs, and their guns.

        G   D
In your head, in your head they are crying.

CHORUS

        E5   C5   G5   D5
In your head, in your head, zombie, zombie, zombie, hey, hey.

                  E5   C5   G5   D5
What's in your head, in your head, zombie, zombie, zombie, hey, hey, hey?

VERSE

Emi   Cmaj7   G   D
Another mother's breakin' heart is taking over.

Emi   Cmaj7   G   D
When the violence causes silence, we must be mistaken.

       Emi   Cmaj7   G   D
It's the same old theme since nineteen-sixteen. In your head, in your head they're still fighting,

         Emi   Cmaj7
With their tanks, and their bombs, and their bombs, and their guns.

        G   D
In your head, in your head they are dying.

CHORUS

        E5   C5   G5   D5
In your head, in your head, zombie, zombie, zombie, hey, hey.

                  E5   C5   G5   D5
What's in your head, in your head, zombie, zombie, zombie. Hey, hey, hey?